PUPPETJI'S
Words of Wizdumb

Deeply Meaningless Insights and Revelations

By

Master Puppetji Guru

DEDICATION

I dedicate this book to my beloved late teacher, Sri Sri Onandonanandana: the Guru who talked a lot but never said much. Thank you for helping me see the truth beyond words, beyond meaning, and beyond the mystery. You showed me the light at the end of the tunnel…which was really the search and rescue team come to find me when I got lost that one time playing in the catacombs. Thank you for showing me that an apple a day eventually just makes you sick of apples, and that humor and laughter are truly the best medicine.

CONTENTS

ACKNOWLEDGMENTS

This book would not be possible if it weren't for every single person who has ever crossed my path, including but not limited to: artists, dancers, wizards, magicians, scientists, doctors, philosophers, yogis and yoginis, homeless people, cooks, writers, clowns, and mimes…all leading me to this moment. But as you read this, that moment I just spoke of has passed and I have probably met more bizarre and wonderful people since then. So I acknowledge all of you as well. To those I haven't yet met or who haven't purchased my book, I must regrettably leave you out of these acknowledgments.

Introduction

Welcome to my first book, Puppetji's Words of Wizdumb: a free-range, non-GMO, gluten-free paperback retreat for your soul.

I contemplated many subtitles for this collection of socksangs from around the world. "Beyond the Beyond" was one, but that felt too much like a book about talking to dead people. I don't talk to dead people, or dead pets. I ultimately settled on "Deeply Meaningless Insights and Revelations." It is multi layered - like a tasty Rum wedding cake with whipped crème and strawberries. In non-dual terms: When we go beyond meaning, we become the experience of nothing. My hope is that the words in this book will help you pull back the curtain from the illusion and experience some wizdumb behind the mystery, some humor in your every day interactions. And maybe giggle at just how serious your spiritual practice has become. It's time to *Enlighten-Up*.

Gratitude is attitude with a thank you and a please,
But attitude with out gratitude is like pizza without the
cheese.

~ Master Puppetji

Do not do as I do, nor do as others do. That's a lot of do-do. And we all know what That smells like…

~Master Puppetji

NOTHINGNESS

On my recent travels, I have encountered many beings from all walks of life who are questioning their Purpose and Existence. The common thread seems to be that the cause of all our suffering is addiction. Yes, there are those who are addicted to the porn, the drugs and reality television. But Puppetji knows the truth: the real drug is the mind.

This is why we have mantras, why we dance and practice yoga...and occasionally smoke from the sacred hookah. Yoga is more than doing postures in a class; though DOWNWARD DOGGIE is most pleasing to my hamstrings, yoga is a way of life in which one gently moves one's attention from the head to the heart. This does not have to be a difficult endeavor; it can be as easy and rewarding as transferring money from your checking account into Puppetji's sacred donation bowl.

When we dance in the Unknown, the divine moment - the NOW – we come to realize that all is as it is, and that is all there is, and you and I are that which is, and That is That.

This is what you are: NO THING. That's right, you are Nothing and that's something. A play on words? Perhaps, but Puppetji suggests that peace lies not in our past or in our future, as these concepts are illusions created by the mind. Peace, love, and freedom cannot be found by following our addictive patterns, for these are but temporary remedies for that which has no meaning and needs no cure. You will never find that which you seek in any thing outside your temple…or someone else's temple…or Shirley Temple. YOU are that which you seek. Stop the search and remember:

You are not special. You are not important. You are LOVE - and Love is everything.

NEVER MIND

The mind is filled with chaos and confusion. Do not listen to this chatter. Rather, be silent. Stop the search for reasons why things are as they appear, for all is an illusion created by the mind, only to confuse, like a dog chasing its tail. Know this:

You will never figure it out – and there is nothing to figure out.

Put an end to this mental filibuster. When we are quiet, when we stop what we are doing and bask in the golden glow of nothingness, only then do we glimpse a glimmer of the truth of who we really are: the unfathomable, infinite mystery; the deep, calm pool from which all life blossoms. The space-no space between the inhale and the exhale. Between pleasure and pain. You are that which allows all to be possible. You are possibility itself. But don't take my word for it - I don't even exist. I know nothing and nothing that I say means anything anyway.

SEEING

What do you see? Who is seeing?
You think you are seeing and yet in truth, seeing is
happening. YOU are not seeing, for YOU do not exist.
You may believe you are seeing what you think you see
but that is merely the identity watching a movie made of
memories…step back: Who sees? Who is seeing? You
see? Actually…you don't see. See?

ONE

Society and culture say that we are separate, that you are There and I am Here. That you have something that I want or I have something that you need and I won't give it up. Much fighting and wars and conflicts ensue. But in truth, I am you and you are me. There is only ever ONE. And we may know this to be true, yet we still can't get along. What the fuck is that about? Puppetji believes this is so because there is a fighting or a war or a conflict going on inside each "one" of us that is merely being reflected in the world. Make peace inside, my friends. Only then will we be able to share our toys.

YOGA

I don't like the modern yoga. It has become the Starbucks of spiritual practice. Who pays nineteen dollars to stand like a mountain – and three freaking fifty for a black cup of coffee? Besides, every yoga class I have been to is so freaking crowded and sweaty and there's always the lady with too much perfume, trying to mask her diet of garlic and onions, or that cocktail she had before class… and the guy who farts and sneezes and burps like a monkey every time he gets in downward dog. Really? Do you have to? And don't even get me started on the see-thru yoga pants, for Buddha's sake, no thank you. I can have my coffee and my yoga at home in peace, and for quite a hell of a lot less. Plus, I can watch Dr. Phil at the same time.

Yesterday is history, tomorrow is a mystery and today is a gift. That is why it is called the present…and also why I didn't get you anything for your birthday.

~Master Puppetji

WHAT IS SACRED?

In a word: Everything. All is sacred. Like my non-dual friend Tony Parsons once said, "Whether you are in deep meditation on the top of a mountain, or having coffee in the city with your mother or a prostitute, or engaging in mind-blowing, kinky tantric sex with a warm mango, or taking a dump in the woods with no toilet paper in sight…all is sacred." And that my friends is the whole poop and nothing but the poop.

DANCE

Oh, how I love the ecstatic dance: the moving meditation. Sweating my prayers, dancing like everyone is watching and then showering like I've never been wet. It's like my good friend Ram Dass once said when we were doing sacred plant ceremony in the desert: "If you don't shake your Buddha, your ass will turn to Gouda." Wise words. Actually, now that I think about it, I may have said those words-but they came out of Ram's third eye. Crazy, I tell you. Dancing between shadow and light on a dance floor made of stars-good times.

COMPLAINING

I do not understand this dilemma. You complain of spicy food yet continue to use sriracha, yes? You see, complaining only perpetuates that which you focus on, creating more and more things to complain about. Stop. Be silent. As my good buddy Osho once said, "If you don't got nothing good to say, then please, shut the fuck up and make me a chai tea."

GOSSIP

This gossip thing is a childish way in which the immature aspects of the unenlightened mind unsuccessfully justifies one's superiority over others, which in turn merely mask one's own deep insecurities. So Puppetji doesn't recommend it. By the way, did you hear that Oprah is adopting a dog with only one leg? Apparently she thinks that this pet will ultimately bring her Hoppiness…

ENLIGHTENMENT

Enlightenment is so overrated; nothing to achieve. Merely awakening from the Dream. Shining a light on the illusion, revealing the truth – that all is an illusion – which doesn't necessarily make life any easier. Enlightenment is the experience of the deep knowing…that you don't know anything. You awaken from an apparent nightmare and turn on the LIGHT, only to see all the monsters hiding under your bed. Like my good friend Gangaji says, "You can either be a chicken shit mother fracker and run away, or you can look your monsters in the eye and say, Hey - Let's Party."

THE SECRET

Okay…What is the big freaking secret? Basic quantum physics people, the Law of Attraction. Besides, everybody's talking about The Secret so I guess it's not a big secret anymore. And it's definitely no secret that in order to get the answer to the Secret- it's gonna cost you 29 freaking 95 for the DVD. Very expensive secret. But I must say…you CAN have anything that you want. But WHO wants?? Who is wanting? Who desires the need to want? Who wants and desires the need to want to be needy and to desire something that it really doesn't need and only thinks it wants?? The ego!! The truth of who you are wants nothing, needs nothing, is nothing. So getting the new car, the new house, or the supermodel wife all are merely feeding the ego and will not bring you happiness. The desire to have more things only serves to perpetuate the grand illusion, therefore creating more desire to want more and more things that you really can't afford, ultimately leading to bankruptcy…and then more suffering and more desire to not suffer. This is the truth - and you can read more about it for only $19.95 if you order my book by midnight tonight. Operators are standing by.

You are being puppeteered by the hand of your history.

~ **Master Puppetji**

WORLD PEACE

Oh yes…world PEACE!!! Everybody wants world peace, but nobody is willing to walk the walk and not just simply talk some talk, like absent-minded beauty pageant contestants. Yes, you see? As my old college roommate party buddy Nisargadatta once said, "You are not in the world, the world is in you." All that you think you see is merely a reflection of your own inner world.

Stop. Sit. Close your eyes. Feel the warm smile of peace spreading across your face, moving down inside, until every organ in your body has a smile on it. You are one big freaking smiling organism vibrating and emanating love into the cosmos.   This is how you change the world: YOU smile and the world smiles with you.

ARE YOU A PUPPET?

Are you a puppet? Do you feel like you are being animated by unseen forces? Making you do and say crazy, stupid things? Who or what is puppeteering you?

You are neither the puppet, nor the puppeteer. And yet, you are also both. The animated and the animator. In truth, you are the animation – or that which allows the animation to occur.

The immeasurable force that moves all... IS all.

We go through most of our lives being blindly puppeteered by the hand of our history. To be truly free, we must pull the hand of history out of our individual and collective ass. As the wise wooden boy Pinocchio once said, " We must cut the strings of our history and run." Of course, this will work better if you are a marionette - if you are a hand puppet, pull out the hand-parasite that lives within...then, run like hell.

YOU ARE DREAMING

As the old saying goes, "Row, row, row your boat gently down the stream …life is but a dream." If this is so, who is dreaming? And where did I get this boat?

You see, you are not the dreamer or the dream, but rather dreaming itself.

You are….dreaming.

Another example might be:

You are not the seer, nor the seen, but seeing itself.

You are …seeing.

Get it?? You see???...Well, okay, if you still don't get it…..another example might be:

You are not the hearing or the heard…unless you are a cow.

ATTACHMENT VS. NON-ATTACHMENT

What is all this chatter about non-attachment? Let's face it: we are attached. We are attached to our things and our stuff. We are attached to the body-mind game. We are attached to people, our favorite yoga pants...and states of being. So what?

Who said attachment was a bad thing in need of correction? Hmmm? There is nothing wrong. All is as it is and that is it. We are all, which means that even what we perceive as negative is always embraced by the Beloved. There is nothing to change, nothing to fix, nowhere to go, and nothing to do because all is love – and love is all. How many times does Puppetji have to say this?? Hmmm? But I must warn you: don't get too attached to your attachments, for they are transient illusions, coming and going, and ultimately they will not bring you happiness. And if you are so focused on the idea of non-attachment that you become attached to your beliefs about non-attachment, well my friends, then you're right back where you started...attached.

FANTASY

Love is often times associated with some sort of utopian "happily-ever-after." This is not Love-this is fantasy.

My friends - stop this Nonsense.

You are addicted to a freaking fairy tale. The handsome prince on the white horse will not come to save the day with a white picket fence and an overflowing bank account. (But if he did, that would be totally hot, yes?)

Okay, so you get lost in this manmade illusion of the Dream Come True. Until one day you WAKE UP. Maybe you come home from your yoga retreat to find your fat ass Prince Charming watching Jerry Springer while chugging beers and snarfing down pizza (and to top it off, the Prince hasn't emptied the trash in the bathroom for over a month. And his clipped toenails are all over the floor.) Now what do you do? The Prince is a bum, yes? Well I'll tell you what you do. You toss the lazy, unemployed, good-for-nothing bum of a Prince out on his ass, that's what. Game over!

But maybe you don't learn. Maybe you are still searching, because then you get all hot and horny for your yoga instructor. After all, he's successful, vegetarian, has his own hair, is in great shape, and has a nice bike. Sweet package, yes?? STOP. WAKE UP! No one, no "other" can fill you, for you are full and complete just as you are. YOU are that which you seek. Once you realize this, the search is over; sacred relationship will find you.

Just be the love that you already are and the love you think you need to seek will find you for you are already here waiting for yourself to show up and love yourself but you forgot to let yourself know you were coming - this is why we have email and texting...You see?

AND...once free from the illusion of Happily Ever After, you will most assuredly have the best mind-body-soul-blowing sex of your life.

EASTER

Ah yes, the Easter. Very special day for a lot of people in pastel hats. The colored eggs, the jelly beans, the chocolate bunnies that love to reproduce, yes? 'Tis a celebration of the day the Buddha came out of the cave and saw his shadow and we had three more freaking months of winter. Alas, this is merely a made up story passed down through the ages. Easter is really a Pagan celebration of the coming of Spring and the fertility of the Earth, honoring the great Pagan fertility goddess Ester (which was later changed to Easter by the Christians). That is why we associate the eggs and the bunnies with this day: fertility. And with the flowers and the birds and the bees all blooming and pollinating and having kinky sex, this is why we all feel so frisky and horny, yes? Puppetji believes it was the great poet Rumi who once said: "The best part of Easter is, it signifies the warm blossoming of opportunity – for all to go party in Mexico and Florida." The mystics sure did love the Spring Break.

PUPPETJI'S DAILY MORNING AFFIRMATION FOR PEOPLE OVER 40

I am gratitude. I am smiling and filled with abundant love.
I vibrate this gratitude and love to everyone and
everything in the world. My DNA, stool, and urine
sparkle with light. I have great joint mobility, non-saggy
boobs, or even if they do sag below my knees…I'm okay
with it. I have no halitosis. Night sweats are just
reminders of when I used to swim in the nasty dirty
waters of the river Ganga. It's all good. I am healthy,
strong, and beautiful. No worries or stress. Positivity
pulses through my still-beating heart. I am alive, sexy,
and sparkly. And when people see how vibrant and clear
I am, I remind them that I am merely a divine reflection
of their own beauty and light…and that if they buy me
lunch, I'll show them the tattoo on my ass that I got when
I was 20.

How can we know what we don't even know we don't know?

~Master Puppetji

MEDITATION

Yes of course, if you go to the top of the mountain, or the Ashram, or the middle of the desert – a place with no distractions – you can find peace and quiet. But if, like Puppetji, you live in the city, can you still find inner peace amidst all the distractions?

Let us quiet our minds for a moment –just notice all the sounds. The birds, the fire truck, the construction, the homeless guy arguing with himself, that fly, the hot neighbors having loud, crazy, tantric, kinky, mind-blowing sex next door, the gun shots. Merely part of the fabric of our lives, yes? Let go of any distracting thoughts, you can clean the toilet later…for it is not about the thoughts my friends; it is about the space between the thoughts… Focus on your breath. Notice the sensations in your body. Ahhh yes. Beautiful. You did it. Now, use this sacred, peaceful space as a touchstone throughout your day. See your life as a moving, walking, talking meditation. Things will always be happening around us that we have no control over – but what we can control through practice is how we react to these things. Okay, now go clean that toilet; it's starting to smell.

KIRTAN

Many people ask me: Puppetji – you are such a popular online guru, with videos seen in over 85 countries, you have so many followers and fans and devotees, you share so much wisdom about love and togetherness and laughter and garum masala - so why have I never seen you at a Kirtan? Do you not like to sing and dance and chant and be devotional like the rest of us? Do you think you are better than us, by being separate? What gives, Puppetji - what is your freaking problem?

First of all, I must say this: I am not separate from you – I am your own inner guru manifested in this form so that you can be reminded that you are indeed constantly being operated by the hand of your history. Secondly, I am you and you are me – we are one – so if you think I'm not wherever you are, look again. Hello, hi.

Now, about the Kirtan: Puppetji loves to sing and dance and get his devotional groove on just as much as the next guru. But he has trouble remembering all the words – that's why he prefers Karaoke Kirtans. You can see all the words on the screen – you can even have a little bouncing Ohm to help you with the rhythm of the thing, so much fun. Why is this not a national phenomenon? Maybe a new reality show: SO YOU THINK YOU CAN KIRTAN. Yes?

LOVE

We love to talk about love: I love this – I love that. She loves me, he loves me not. I am head over heels in love. But do we really know anything about love? Hmmm?

Love is merely a word with many definitions. There is unconditional love, romantic love, and platonic love. Holy love, self-love, tantric love, shamanic love. You got the Polyamory love thing going around – which is basically: Polly wants more than one cracker, then you have tennis love (to keep score love/30).

But the love I speak of is beyond definition - beyond fantasy, ecstasy, and heartbreak.

When we speak of being "in love" with someone or something, we are merely stating our deep affection for this person or thing. And yet, this fleeting emotion can be altered in the blink of an eye. You think you love this person or thing, then you see a movie or commercial or read *50 Shades of Gray* and Boom - your idea of what you thought was love goes right out the window. We have been manipulated and hypnotized to continuously seek out another object to love. The ONE – the perfect love-soul mate, who doesn't fart or chew with her mouth open, or clip his toenails on the floor. Romantic, yes?

It's like when you go to a restaurant and you order the chicken masala, and then you're eating it and it's delicious – but the guy at the table next to you got the chicken tikka – and you think, "maybe I should have got the pasta or some sushi" (which is crazy because you're in an Indian restaurant).

Nonsense, I tell you.

You see, the Lover of your dreams is not coming on the white horse to sweep you up and save the day…and bring you some butter…

The love of your life is YOU - right here, right now, this moment - you are the chicken tikka you seek …you are your own Lover, muse, soul mate, you are your own destiny. You ARE love…so stop seeking.

I believe it was Rumi who once said, "The grass may appear to be greener on the other side – but somebody still gotta mow that lawn and pull the weeds." Well, maybe it was Dr. Seuss.

Now, I know what you're thinking: but Puppetji, what if they got astro turf – then nobody gotta mow the lawn? Okay, you got me there; that's a good one.

Look, the bottom line is this, my friends: romance, infatuation, lust, and hot, crazy, tantric, mind-blowing, kinky sex – are all fleeting and temporary. True love is a divine experience that is unwavering, constant, and only found in the present moment. Mystics and shamans and poets and musicians and homeless people have written about love for centuries, and all I can say for sure is this: I have no idea what the hell I am talking about…so let's all just enlighten up.

THE SELF

What is this notion of the self anyway? Can the self be selfless? If there is only one self, can there be your self and my self…hmmm?

What is the self? Who is the self? Who wants to know? Who is asking? Does the self know itself? If the self fell in a forest, would it hear itself fall? Would it know; would it care? If the self met itself on the street, would it recognize itself, or think it was someone else? Like that crazy drug addict who stole my bike outside a coffee shop? Hmmmm?

Now I know what you're thinking: but Puppetji, what the fuck are you talking about?

Well, let me just ask this – who wants to know?

If you don't get off your mat and shake your Buddha,
your ass will turn to Gouda.

~Master Puppetji

SOCKSANG Q&A

STUDENT
Puppetji, you are an enlightened master, self-realized, and so on. You have so many beautiful women around you all the time, an entourage of sensuality. How do you deal with temptation?

PUPPETJI
Hmmmmmm. This falls into the area of attraction and repulsion. Puppetji does not know of temptation, only BEING. When you try to push away or grasp for what the mind desires, you create suffering. Stop, be still, and the light of your true essence will guide you back to where you have never left. Where you are, where you is...the incredible "IS-ness". Through being and not doing...by tracking the sensations in your body and only observing, you will see the unseen and know the unknown...that you are nothing, you are unimportant, you are not special and when all is said and done, at the end of the day, when you are apparently dead and have returned to a mere measly pile of dust in the wind...you will look back on your life with humility and discover that nobody really gave a flying crap anyway.

STUDENT
Puppetji, I have been studying the non-dual teachings. The more I come to understand these principles, the less I seem to know. I feel like I am disappearing. I can't sleep, work or eat. Can you help?

PUPPETJI

You have over identified and are lost in a blockbuster movie in your mind. Leave this sticky-floored theatre in your head and go for a walk on the beach. Sit. You must realize that through stillness, you are the source of all that is. You are love and there is nothing else but love. Patience and Forgiveness are key; your hunger for the truth will be your guide. Speaking of hungry, did you see that movie ALIVE, where the plane crashes in the mountains and the survivors get so hungry, they eat each other like beef jerky? Yes? This is what you must do: find a cave, or a mountain. Sit in silence until the hunger is so unbearable that you begin to eat your leg, until finally you have devoured your own flesh, leaving nothing but your bones. This will be challenging, but only then will you come to realize that you are the creator of your own reality. Quantum physics, my friend. AND.... you taste like chicken. AND God loves you.

STUDENT

Master Puppetji, What is the meaning of Life?

PUPPETJI

Ah, yes – the question of all questions. Life has no meaning. It is what you make of it. What it means to you may be different from your neighbor. It is a subjective concept and each individual can make up their own answer to this question in attempts to give their life some sort of meaning. Based on their needs and desires. Meaning is merely a made up word used to create meaning for the word "meaning." When in truth, there is no meaning. You see what I mean? Of course not-it's all meaningless. Likewise, things we see are actually not as they appear. We have all been hypnotized into believing - that is a chair, that is a table, a floor, a window, that this is a tablecloth.

And similarly, we each hypnotize others around us into believing what we want them to see – based on fear and, of course, our own personal history.

For instance, I am not really a Guru. Through our collective conditioning, I show you what I want you to see and you see what you want to see and together we create the image of Puppetji. Oh, I just made a rhyme.

Everyone is so focused on the meaning of life when there are bigger questions: Who are we, really? Why do we do what we do and say what we say? What are words? What is language? All made up to create a false sense of safety...of identity. And what is a name but merely a word used to create an identity, which is false by its very nature. What is this identity we are so attached to? Who is attached?
Who wants to know? What is suffering...who suffers? Where did all these words and language and questions come from?

I am no Doctor Phil, or Amma, or Tony Danza, but I know we cannot claim ownership of words. Though words themselves are irrelevant and meaningless, they can be guideposts to truth, for all is what it is and that is it. And Just THIS for all. You see? By making it an inquiry, you will find that you can go beyond the limits of the words' apparent meaning...from the known to the unknown. The truth cannot be known, only experienced.

I share with you the wisdom of my Guru and his Guru, and his Guru's Guru, and his Guru's Guru's Guru:

There is nothing to do, and nowhere to go. You were never born and will therefore never die. Death is an illusion, as is birth, and your perception of what you believe to be real. Is the goal not happiness, aliveness, and peace for all? Until we realize that all is found and never has been lost, or rather that all is...and that we are all...that we ARE that which we seek, we will be bound by the illusions of suffering, sadness, and loss.

Let go of the ME- MINE. Let go of the search for the Holy Grail. You are the sacred chalice that you seek. Seek only the courage to go beyond what you think you know and you will leave behind the limits of your knowledge. You must unlearn and forget this nonsense. Question everything. Shift your gaze inward, towards the light. The movie is over – and yet, there is no end but only an ocean of endless beginnings. Puppetji wishes to remind you to find your freedom in the dance of the unknown. Awaken your inner fool for the fool will set you free. Laughter will brighten your days. As my foolish master Sri Sri Onandonandonandondonna said to me right before he had a fatal massive coronary, "Let's put some more gravy on those mashed potatoes." He heartily enjoyed his Last Supper.

You complain of dirty dishes, and yet you continue to use a dirty sponge. Get a new sponge!

~Master Puppetji

ABOUT THE AUTHOR

Puppetji is the only living master made of foam. He is a host, Guru, public speaker, joyologist & momentarian.

His insightful and useless video "Socksangs" have been seen in over 85 countries. His Wizdumb talks are light-hearted reminders that help us open our eyes to a new way of SEEING. A master at squashing illusion with Wizdumb, humor and meaningless insights, Puppetji cuts through the spiritual mumbo-jumbo and gets right to The Truth: According to Puppetji.

Considered to be one of our last great-enlightened masters, Puppetji selflessly delivers his meaningless words of Wizdumb to anyone who will listen and even those who don't.

Puppetji's message is simple: You take life too seriously...Enlighten-up!

When Puppetji isn't demystifying dogma, karma, dharma, yoga, or busy practicing the art of nothingness, he helps run the family store in Pune, India: The New Delhi Deli; home of the famous six foot Swami-Pastrami.

SPECIAL THANKS

To my editor Bonnie Solomon. Maurizio and Zaya, Michael Divine, Ratna "Apple Tree", Jerrold, Amanda, All my Kevins and the Murray Clan.

www.ingramcontent.com/pod-product-compliance
Lightning Source LLC
Chambersburg PA
CBHW042120060426
42446CB00038B/14